Six-Word Lessons to

CREATE STELLAR TEAMS

100 Lessons to Drive
Your Teams to Success

Thomas Tomasevic

Published by Pacelli Publishing
Bellevue, Washington

Six-Word Lessons to Create Stellar Teams

All rights reserved. No part of this book may be reproduced or transmitted in any form or by any means, electronic or mechanical including photocopying, recording or by any information storage or retrieval system, without the written permission of the publisher, except where permitted by law.

Limit of Liability: While the author and the publisher have used their best efforts in preparing this book, they make no representation or warranties with respect to accuracy or completeness of the content of this book. The advice and strategies contained herein may not be suitable for your situation. Consult with a professional when appropriate.

Copyright © 2015, 2017 by Thomas Tomasevic

Published by Pacelli Publishing
9905 Lake Washington Blvd. NE, #D-103
Bellevue, Washington 98004
Pacellipublishing.com

Cover and interior design by Pacelli Publishing
Author photo by PintoPortrait.com
Cover photo by Shutterstock, used with permission

ISBN-10: 1-933750-46-4
ISBN-13: 978-1-933750-46-0

Foreword

Team development is an inexhaustible topic for me. I get passionately pulled into building teams, making them effective, efficient, harmonious, focused, and well-structured. I enjoy dealing with team dynamics, coaching, and seeing progress and improvements in performance. This is why my company, T2 Team consulting (T2Team.com), based near Seattle, Washington, is focused on team development, including leadership, team analysis, and dynamics.

Putting all that passion into the Six-Word Lessons format was a challenge. Many of the topics had to be distilled down to the most pragmatic advice. As you read the book, know that the suggestions written in this book are based on 20+ years of personal experience as well as the teachings of several team dynamics researchers whose insights and solutions I use in my practice.

Acknowledgements

I want to thank all my clients who make it possible for me to practice what I enjoy. I hope that my involvement is useful to them and that they enjoy the "lasting results" I try to achieve for them.

I want to thank my partners from Resource Associates Corporation and SYMLOG Consulting Groups, who provide me with technology to offer efficient and effective solutions to my clients. I also want to thank my business partner, Leigh Yafa, who was always there to offer editing skills, suggestions, and advice essential for my work and wellbeing.

Table of Contents

A Few Words About Team Basics 7

Goal Setting is Key for Success 19

Attitude Drives 80% of Team's Success 29

Core Team Management Concepts and Tasks 35

Optimizing Team Performance: What and How 47

Responsibilities, Methods in Motivating Your Team 55

Communication: Bloodline of a Good Team 59

Ensuring Alignment Between Achievements and Rewards 67

Establishing and Nurturing Optimal Team Culture 75

Building New Teams: Do's and Don'ts 83

What Every Team Leader Must Know 91

Leadership Through Values: Effectiveness of "Valueship" 101

Understanding Various Team Types and Stages 107

Keeping Teams Informed Through Team Meetings 119

"Coming together is a beginning. Keeping together is progress. Working together is success."

~~ Henry Ford

A Few Words About Team Basics

You are here, that is fine.

You have probably picked up this book because you are curious about building great teams. If that curiosity comes from being a part of a dysfunctional team, that's alright. See, current dysfunctions are not a determinant of the team's future. You can work with any team and lessen or eradicate the dysfunction by focusing on the positive influencers in the team dynamics.

Main differences between groups and teams

Groups share similar goals, but do not work together as a unit. Think of a sales team--the members work toward the joint quota, but don't necessarily help each other to achieve it. Teams share the same goals and help each other achieve those goals.

The importance of understanding team dynamics

Having great team dynamics is not just a goal. It is a necessity. Don't confuse the two. Few companies will reward you for having a great team, but every company will reward great results. However, your team will be more likely to achieve goals if team members get along and work well together.

Understand your and your team's needs.

Try to understand your motivations and your team's needs: Do you need to improve your team? Are you leading a stagnant team? Was your team recently formed? Do team members understand the team's charter, roles and responsibilities? Or are you just interested in knowing more about team effectiveness?

Imagine and visualize your perfect team.

Envision building a highly productive, forward thinking, excited team that can achieve anything; or a harmonious team that manages itself; or a contented yet creative team that is able to take direction and criticism. Which of these teams appeals to you and your environment's needs?

Clarify your team's mission and purpose.

What is your team's objective? Has the objective been fully defined, shared, discussed and accepted by the team? Take the time to review past, current and future objectives with the team. Work with the team to understand what is ahead, what defines success, and how it will be rewarded.

Has the team's mission changed recently?

Put the differences between past and future objectives in perspective and help the team understand what behavioral changes are needed to achieve new objectives. Explain what new expertise is needed (if any), and how future teams will go about accomplishing the tasks. Remember, involve the team in the discussion, and sell your ideas where necessary.

Is expectation to deliver creative solutions?

It is important to define up front if the team's objective is to be creative in delivering results, or is status quo, structure, timeline or cost most important? If creativity is expected and rewarded, are there any areas to focus on and/or leave alone? Be clear in setting expectations and boundaries.

Success may depend on external support.

Ask questions and look for ambiguity or hesitation: Does the team have the freedom and empowerment necessary to accomplish the team's mission? For example, is reporting relationship and accountability set up in a way to make success possible and likely? What are external dependencies that remain outside of the team's control?

10

Finally, what makes a team successful?

Success is the result of achieving or exceeding goals. Properly set, clear, and well-communicated goals are critical. Other success-driving components are: the team's skill and knowledge, workflow and, most importantly, attitudes. Skills are yours to find and develop, and they are task specific. We will take a look at goals and attitudes in the following chapters.

Six-Word Lessons to Create Stellar Teams

Goal Setting is Key for Success

Focus on obstacles; fully understand them.

Identify all of the current obstacles and pinpoint the issues, processes, and tendencies that stand in the way of creating the team culture you desire. Focus on the job functions, not on individual team members. If you have a hard time identifying the obstacles, explain your team's workflow to a trusted advisor and have him/her ask questions.

Set goals, tasks, dates and ownership.

Once you know what you want to achieve, create an inventory of your goals. Break down goals into actionable tasks. Identify the obstacles you may face. Then list workarounds and solutions. Assign the tasks to owners, including due dates, including yourself. Have owners commit to delivering by the due date and keep them accountable.

Do you trust the new plan?

Once you have broken down your goals into tasks, obstacles, owners and dates, ask yourself if you have any doubts about achieving the goal. If so, identify what is causing you angst, and rework the plan. Are there external dependencies? If so, take on the ownership of working with external dependencies. You will be need to align them with your team's needs.

Set clear mission, priorities and goals.

As a team leader, your absolute highest goal is to do what will keep the team most effective. Remind yourself that effectiveness is measured by achieving and exceeding business results. To achieve the business goals, you need to analyze them, understand them, accept them, explain them, and keep the team focused in reaching them.

Talk about it: motivate your team.

As a leader, you are expected to lead by example--work on your conviction first. Once you are convinced that you have a solid plan, share your confidence with others. Your confidence will motivate the team. Share your thinking process and data (if any) and ask for support if necessary.

ID: 16

Adjust your plan and be flexible.

Successful leadership is situational. Never lose touch with the environment: stay involved, alert and flexible. Revisit your goals inventory whenever you get new information, data or insights. Do so as you go through this book, as well. Some ideas and solutions may surface and you should update the plan accordingly.

Every team member understands the mission.

Make sure all team members understand the team's mission, including their own accountability in making the mission successful, and that they know how to get there. Once they understand what they need to do, ask them to verbalize what they need from others (this comes easy), and what they will deliver to others. Every expectation should have an owner.

Obstacles are not to be feared.

Calling out possible obstacles and identifying workarounds disempowers doubt. So, try to identify them during the planning phase. Don't be afraid of finding too many obstacles. When you identify all obstacles you can think of (involve the team in this process as needed), work on a plan on how to address each and every one of them.

Practice of setting team-wide goals

A team has to have an identity (i.e., "We are a team of mouse-trap engineers") and a purpose (i.e., "We build the best mouse traps"). This ideate and the team's goals are interchangeable. Setting goals means applying the team's purpose on the individual level by developing personal tasks. Ask team members to explain how they contribute to the team's identity.

Attitude Drives 80% of Team's Success

Importance of attitude in team play

Attitude is 80 percent of success. Attitude determines if a team's individual hard work, skills and knowledge will result in positive or negative results. Attitude comes from within, and is a minimum requirement for team membership. If there is an attitude problem with a specific team member, identify if the team member in question is the right fit for your team.

Analyzing attitude of individual team members

How do you troubleshoot a team member's attitude? Always review the basics: Does the individual want to be on the team? Are the structure, responsibilities, rewards and boundaries properly set and accepted by the team member? Is attitude a reflection of a specific situation or does it reflect on personality? Are there unknown conflicts on the team?

Addressing negative attitudes of team members

If you conclude that a team member does not want to be on the team, does not want to cooperate with the rest of the team, or thrives on negativity, all you can do as team lead is to explain the expectation and consequences, then act in the best interest of the team.

Improving attitudes of overlooked team members

This is not to say that you can never help. If an individual's negative attitude comes from feeling underutilized, overlooked, overworked, or underappreciated, you should address the issues. Be clear about what you will do and what you expect in return.

Great individuals can make great teams.

Put great minds together, and you will end up with a winning solution, right? Usually, but not always. Even "great minds" need to agree to work together. They need to recognize and respect others' roles, capabilities, and contributions first. Often, teams of average performers, working together in harmony, will achieve more than groups of exceptional ones. In most cases attitude, not intelligence, is key.

Core Team Management Concepts and Tasks

A great team can manage itself.

A great team that understands the team's objectives will be largely self-managing and self-correcting. So where does that leave the manager? Usually a manager would just do minute adjustments to direction and external communication. As the environment changes, the manager owns the responsibility of communicating the changes and adjusting the course.

Great teams always agree on everything.

Far from it! Great teams have healthy dynamics that encourage respectful differences of opinion and looking for the best solutions. It's a "give and take" dynamic. The goal is to encourage new ideas and "outside-the-box" thinking while rewarding good teamwork and, of course, results.

Should teams agree on most things?

Yes. The team has to share the vision, and thus should come to an agreement on how to deliver a unified solution. Just as too much disagreement is unhealthy, watch for too much agreement, as it may indicate that the team does not think creatively. Likewise, beware of consistent "devil's advocates" as they will eventually be rejected by the team as "nay-sayers."

Well-oiled teams can run forever.

I wish. Well-oiled teams certainly deliver a lot more than squeaky teams. Because they like working together, harmonious teams enjoy what they do, and are able to run longer distances. But in the excitement of winning, such teams sometimes suffer from burnout.

Dealing with burnout on your team

Projects often require extraordinary efforts in certain phases of the project. This can cause burnout. Watch for grumpiness, lack of élan, and a rise in conflicts where there were few previously, especially after periods of great activity. These are external signs of burnout. Prevent burnout by allowing for some downtime between projects.

Celebrate success; share recognition; gain effectiveness.

Developing an effective team requires a long-term commitment. The team needs to be organized, objectives understood, results achieved, and success celebrated. Instill a sense of confidence, importance, or even greatness through personal and team achievements and successes.

There are good days, bad days.

A team is a living entity. Depending on the situation, it is alright to experience moments of dysfunction even on the best of teams. Most of the time, the dysfunction will be temporary and easily explainable. In most cases, they are easily remedied. Talking issues over, finding middle ground, or giving team members time off if burned out can help.

Who's responsible for training team members?

You, as the team leader, should be involved with creating training agendas even if you are not conducting the training sessions. The training topics should be aligned with team needs and personal interests of team members. Training is also a motivational tool that works with team members interested in expanding their knowledge.

Understand your team's differences and diversity.

Teams are by definition diverse, and the division of tasks causes some specialization. This results in diverse expertise, but maturity, gender, and other differences may be obvious or latent. The lead's task is to create an environment in which differences are understood and accepted. Team building events, diversity tests, etc. help team members recognize and accept differences.

Centralized or decentralized team decision-making

The best teams are enabled to make decisions on the individual level, often with input from the team. The team lead's objective is to enable team-level decision making with adequate involvement of the team lead. The team lead can do this by effectively communicating direction, objectives, and values, then trusting the team with the decision.

How to build trust in teams

Remember that trust is earned: to earn trust from team members, explain objectives and explain how to achieve results. Over time, explain the thinking process and focus on values. Seek and offer insights on how to think through problems, and let the team determine their tasks. Keep yourself accountable in the process and the trust will be mutual.

Optimizing Team Performance: What and How

Great teams are cheaper to run.

This is absolutely true. An old saying is that employees join a new team because of the job description and salary, but stay because of the people. Thus, a happy group will be less focused on the monetary rewards and will experience lower turnover.

How to harmonize many mixed personalities

I recommend personality tests (DISC, MBTI, Animal Types, or others) to keep your team aware of each other's personalities. Why? To help team members realize that there are personal differences in how they operate, and that is OK. If properly taught, DISC tests teach the messenger to communicate in a way that the message receiver can respond quickest and with least resistance.

Need for details; need for speed

Personality tests will reveal a multitude of differences. It is good to recognize that different people have different temperaments, decision-making abilities, levels of patience, interest in details, etc. For example, detail-oriented people need lots of data and, often, time to analyze it. Give them details and then give them time. Quick decision-makers are the opposite.

Team dynamics improve after taking tests.

After administering the personality test of choice, reinforce that recognizing differences in team members' personalities is only the first step. The next step is applying the newly gained knowledge. It is each team member's obligation to understand the audience, and make efforts to deliver messages in a way the audience can easily receive it.

9-5 teams? How about 24-7 teams?

Because of technology, and the fact that people are increasingly relying on an ever-present social media, many teams can communicate outside of the regular working hours. By giving team members freedom from rigid working hours, teams may gain productivity across all hours of the day.

Strengthen cohesion by explaining personal differences.

Strengthen team members' sense of interconnection by teaching them to know themselves and others. Help them see issues from others' perspectives, develop a universally effective communication style, and leverage each other's strengths and weaknesses, while accepting each other as different, unique and valid.

Team's traits to grow and show

Always encourage and help develop team members' self-esteem by listening with empathy and understanding. Encourage their self-confidence, courage to act, self-discipline, positive mental attitude, integrity, and accountability. Remember that self-esteem is a result of success in life. As a leader, you can help team members achieve and recognize their contributions and success.

Responsibilities, Methods in Motivating Your Team

The importance of selling and motivating

Teams always respond best to ideas they buy into. That's why a team's mission, direction, and tasks have to be "sold," not "told." Generously explain the objectives, but don't over-explain how to reach them. If team members understand and accept the general direction, they will fill in the blanks with their own ideas, which will motivate them.

Three ways to motivate the team

There are three general ways to motivate a team: through incentive motivation ("If you do this, you will be rewarded."), consequence motivation ("If you do/don't do this, there will be consequences."), and attitude motivation (giving them opportunities to do more).

How to ensure direction is understood

Communicate the direction to the team. Be clear about objectives, expectations, roles, timelines, etc. Than ask questions and have team members explain back to you: why does the team exist? How will the team's approach benefit the organizational goals? What will be accomplished and why is that relevant?

Communication: Bloodline of a Good Team

Improve the effectiveness of team communication.

Effective communication if often hindered by lack of understanding by the audience. Understanding your team members will help you formulate the message in a way that they "get it" and "accept it" with least resistance. It is up to the person delivering the message to adjust the message in a way that the receiving person can get it most effectively.

Use technology to gain team cohesion.

Our times are blessed with technology that allows 24/7 communication unhindered by time and location. Enable teams to form their own social media presence, share sites, etc. This especially works for the Millennial generation, but will be embraced by other generations once they understand the benefits.

Is social media a team member?

All this talk of social media--how can you benefit from it? Encourage collaboration using Facebook, Instagram, blogs, Skype, etc. Offer training and participate. Define and explain do's and don'ts. Make sure that team members' strengths are leveraged through use of these instant communication channels.

Drawbacks of social media over-communication

Sharing is caring. But, educate your team about sharing information in the responsible way. In the excitement of achieving success, socially active members will want to share details outside of the confines of the team's space. Ensure that the team knows that revealing the team's secrets is not permitted, and as such, is punishable.

Internal and external communication should flow.

The lead's most important task, bar none, is to make sure that information flows effectively. This means that the team is informed and properly understands both external information (expectations, changes) and internal (progress, sequence of tasks, deadlines, handovers, etc.), and that lateral information flow between team members is encouraged, and is working.

Effective communication is expected leader trait.

The leader is expected to offer clear and focused communication, and embody empathy, succinctness, and flexibility. Organize thoughts and speak slowly. Remember that what you say is only a small part of the value listeners get. The majority of communication is in how you say it and who you are.

Ensuring Alignment Between Achievements and Rewards

Reward system to support team focus

For a team to be successful, reward systems need to reward pro-team behavior. Team success must be the main criteria of the reward system. Other rewarded behaviors could include collaboration, making others successful, getting results through teamwork, positive contribution to team morale, etc.

How to objectively evaluate team members

Unless the team manager is immersed in team dynamics, he/she will have a hard time seeing all team members as they are. This is because of the manager's colored/subjective glasses, team members "posing" come reward time, and the simple fact that one person cannot see everything. Rely on feedback from other team members when making reward decisions, or use SYMLOG evaluations.

Financial rewards aren't the only option.

The money your team members earn is not always the most important reward they get out of their jobs. Money is a good thing, but there is more, such as safety, recognition, personal and professional growth, great working conditions, supportive team culture, as well as interesting work. Make sure that you understand your team's individual motivations.

Alternatives to traditional and financial incentives

Material rewards have a tendency to lose effectiveness, often because they are expected, assumed or quickly spent and forgotten. Consider experiential rewards such as travel and adventure. They increase employee loyalty and are part of teambuilding efforts in most companies. They motivate team members and stay in the memory much longer than financial incentives.

Team traits, perception, rewards and consequences

It is good to define and communicate organizational expectations for risk-taking, chain of command, level of ownership, as well as methods for measuring and rewarding performance. Is the rest of the organization excited to support the team, or is the team's existence seen as merely a necessity?

Aspects to consider for team evaluation

To develop teams, evaluate their performance and address any weaknesses. One way to evaluate is to focus on structural strength and behavioral tendencies. Structural analysis looks at the team's ability to perform effective planning, including setting goals and shared vision, decision-making, and innovation of ideas. Behavioral tendencies are evaluated based on interdependent function within teams: conflict management, collaboration, and meeting management.

Establishing and Nurturing Optimal Team Culture

Create an effective problem-solving culture.

To optimize the problem-solving culture of the team, allow for some unconventional ideas, as well as dissent from agreed norms. Some amount of disagreement will be beneficial. This means that the team may feel unfriendly at times, but this will be a necessary aspect of challenging each other's opinions.

Conflict resolution in case of polarization

In case of polarization on the team, look for mediator roles in those who remain friendly with both poles. Coach them to be the in-between person while you find the root cause of the real issues. Always reinforce shared values with the entire team and ask yourself if you are partially responsible for the polarization.

Create coalitions between like-minded members.

Form coalitions on the team. Try to avoid task-based coalitions; rather, focus on value-based coalitions. Use the chain of coalitions to exercise leadership and check if there are breaks in the chain.

Behavior to discourage: no gossip allowed!

Discourage gossip, politics, and cynicism in the team. Neither are welcome, but some managers will try to engage with the team in order to maintain control. Don't follow their example. Have regular check-ins with the team and keep it professional.

Scapegoating in the times of crisis

In times of stress or uncertainty, teams will gang up against a selected scapegoat. Often, the scapegoat is perceived as previously opposing the team's real or perceived values or goals. This scapegoat can be internal or external. Be wary of these situations--they are often unstable and ethically compromising. It is best to defuse the situation without taking sides.

Team-based organization requires cultural change.

Does the organization recognize that the team-based, collaborative, empowering, enabling organizational culture of the future is different than the traditional, hierarchical culture? In order to make a new team-based culture persist and succeed, the organization needs to align raises, portions, bonuses, etc. with the desired culture. Consider both team and individual successes.

Develop an intentional team-specific culture.

Align the purpose of the team with its culture. Encourage and reward behaviors that benefit the team. For example, if the team needs to deliver highly creative results, reward out-of-the-box thinking and risk taking. If the team should deliver consistency, reward process improvements and long-term accountability.

Building New Teams: Do's and Don'ts

How to select appropriate team members

You always want the best of the best employee candidates to fill your team positions, right? Yes and no. Yes, because the best candidates are more effective and are easier to manage. No, because they require premium pay, promotions, and constant challenges. Consider if you are able to offer the environment required by superstars. If so, top candidates are your target.

Dominance should be a shared trait.

Dominance in team members is good, but there should be no big disparity in how dominant each of them are. Encourage those who are more passive or introverted to participate, and discourage anyone who wants to dominate at all times. Remember, dominant team members can make the rest of the team withdraw from decision-making.

Is any size team equally good?

If you want maximum interaction between all members on the team, cap the team size to eight or less. Maximum recommended size of a flat team is eleven team members. Minimum team size, accepted in most industries, is three team members and a lead.

Ensure that team members are committed.

Ask questions and look for ambiguity or hesitation: Do team members want to participate? Do team members agree with the mission and expected outcomes? Is the mission valuable for the company? Will achieving it result in recognition for the team? Are there any growth opportunities on the team? Are team members excited and challenged by the team opportunity?

Are the required competencies properly represented?

State the team's objective or a problem, and then ask questions, looking for ambiguity and hesitation. This will tell you: Are the right people on the team? What are the team's gaps in skills and knowledge? Can the team find a way to get support to fill the gaps--with outside help or training?

All teams go through multiple phases.

Newly formed teams will go through a standard forming, storming, norming and performing process. Team leads can accelerate getting to the performing stage by establishing and explaining roles, responsibilities, and boundaries, as well as development stages for each team member.

A look at roles in teams

Another major factor in developing high-functioning teams is to establish different roles to play and help team members understand them. Roles should be driving (action), coordination (people), and analytical (thought-oriented) roles.

This will give well rounded completeness to the team, and a variety of skills to resort to for a wide variety of situations and objectives.

What Every Team Leader Must Know

Traits that make good team leaders

A team leader is the driver of team culture. He/she leads by example, set rules of acceptable behavior, is consistent, objective, accountable, a clear communicator and motivator, and has the high-level answers. The leader trusts team members, but calls them out if they are out of line. He/she keeps team members focused, and also protects the team members from unnecessary distractions.

The three most common leadership types

Managers can be enhancers, neutralizers or diminishers. Only enhancers build successful teams and can be considered true and effective leaders. Enhancers enjoy adding value to the projects and helping team members grow. They encourage learning and involvement. Enhancers can express genuine emotions. This makes them approachable so teams choose to follow them.

Using positional authority versus earned power

Authority comes from a position a person holds. In general, authority should be used sparingly. Power of influence is earned and can be acquired in any position. Power necessitates trust, authority does not. Only team leads possess both power and authority, yet a powerful team could have multiple members with power.

You as leader: what is leadership?

In my opinion, the best definition of leadership has been voiced by Dwight Eisenhower: "Leadership is the art of getting someone to do something you want done because he or she wants to do it." So, a leader will employ the technique of selling (ideas), motivating, explaining, and mentoring in order to enable the drive and the focus in the team.

Leadership for every situation: situational leadership

Though consistency in leadership is a needed quality, adjusting the style to fit the situation is crucial. At times, team leads are coaches, mentors, teachers, problem solvers, punishers, decision-makers, drivers or followers. Though the leader's style may vary from situation to situation, values, such as integrity, positivity, and accountability are always present.

Leader's dominance: how much is optimal?

A team leader must aim for moderately high dominance in behavior. Overly dominant leaders fail to motivate the team, and passive leaders tend to be seen as checked-out and not caring, thus demotivating the team. A good team leader is not afraid to be in charge, but also listens to and hears the team's opinions.

Does a team leader always lead?

No. A good leader knows when to give space to the others. When you see a leader step back and give someone else the opportunity to lead, it's usually to provide training--to enable others to lead and experience being in the leadership position, or to delegate--to give specific areas of responsibility to individuals or subteams and enable them to self-manage.

Team lead's responsibilities in setting direction

The team lead works with the executive team to define, understand and agree on the direction, and clearly communicate expectations for the team's performance and expected outcomes. Part of the preparation requires vetting organizational commitment to supporting the team with people, time and money. The team members must understand why the team was created.

Six-Word Lessons to Create Stellar Teams

Leadership Through Values: Effectiveness of "Valueship"

Trust is the catalyst of collaboration.

Create an environment of trust and security in which members can push their limits. This is where lessons are learned, creativity flourishes, and bonds are forged. By removing barriers and defensive patterns that operate in day-to-day situations, members become capable of gaining insights unattainable under ordinary circumstances.

Forming new teams around shared values

When forming a team, look for similarities in values between team members. A great difference in values at formation may result in a fractured team. For example, a team that values processes, procedures, and follows chain of command may resist or reject team members who display creativity, individuality and independence.

Reinforcing positive behavior in new teams

Devote your time to helping the team develop values that reinforce productivity, focus on task execution and support friendly behavior. Use crisp communication and a reward system to ensure that everybody understands that you mean it. For example, encourage team members to consider how decisions affect others before they make them.

Reward and discipline your team fairly.

A good business supervisor takes employees seriously. Give praise in public and criticize or reprimand in private. Be fair and explain how reward levels are determined, since even the best team members will have a few blind spots. Likewise, discipline is meant to be a constructive action, and expressing your disapproval is intended to stimulate the positive work attitude.

Six-Word Lessons to Create Stellar Teams

Understanding Various Team Types and Stages

Managing your virtual geo-dispersed teams

As education flourishes globally and information becomes decentralized, it is natural that teams are less and less geo-centric. This makes teams more virtual. Many teams need to adopt 24/7 information flow, decentralized management, and a multi-cultural environment. The manager must set the direction, making sure there are appropriate communication systems and policies in place that support building the appropriate culture on the team.

85

Baby Boomers make good team mentors.

As Baby Boomers (born 1946-1964) exit the workforce, businesses lose tremendous collective experience. Leverage that experience by having part-time mentors from this generation on your team. Studies show that Baby Boomers and Millennials (born 1981-2000s) can be well matched and complement each other by creating a symbiotic relationship: Baby Boomers share experience, Millennials share technological insights.

Millennials expect rewards for team success.

Millennials naturally belong in team environments more than previous generations. Used to nonstop digital interaction, they do well in large communities (virtual or physical). If lacking in people skills and pragmatism, they compensate in collaboration and digital accessibility. Embrace this and leverage it. They bring 24/7 global engagement mentality.

How to lead an experienced team

Your leadership style should ensure that the team is directed strategically and that there are no structural conflicts in the work flow. Give your team the support and encouragement they need. Make sure they have plenty of challenging, interesting work. Clear obstacles out of their path, regardless of whether the obstacles are people or procedures. You want to play the role of coach in this case.

How to lead a motivated team

Your leadership style here is to channel the team's enthusiasm without dampening it. Don't hold them back, but don't let them run off in the wrong direction. Your role is to steer them. Explain the strategy, teach and mentor them, and watch for correctness of decisions and interpersonal conflicts. If there are reasons for your involvement, coach and support rather than slow them down.

How to manage marginally effective teams

In this case, your leadership style should resemble an accountant. Be clear. Track what everyone is doing, such as post-production objectives and quotas. Work with each team member on the expected and achieved progress toward the goals. This will enable you to combat any lack of team accountability yet maintain fairness and objectivity.

Inexperienced teams: a blessing or challenge?

Inexperienced teams can be fun to lead, if you are patient and a good mentor. Such teams are eager, willing, and coachable, but rarely predictable, self-managed, or effective. Thus, the leader of the inexperienced team has to teach and develop the team, and be energized by the team's enthusiasm and progress. Patient and clear management style is often the most effective for such teams.

Best leadership style for difficult teams

Unfortunately, even with great leadership, some teams are difficult to manage. In such teams, the team dynamics will be dismal and results will suffer. The most important thing is to look for the causes of dysfunction. Troubleshooting such teams can be difficult, and I recommend use of SYMLOG to perform a collective 360 where everyone rates everyone else.

Common reasons for dysfunction on teams

A dysfunctional team may be composed of experienced but incompatible or territorial individuals who don't want to work together, usually due to fear, bad attitude or burnout. In such teams, individuals may acquire survival skills that hide their lack of experience, lack of character, or lack of commitment.

Leader's involvement in improving dysfunctional teams

I recommend a 360 evaluation technique to troubleshoot teams. Research SYMLOG and DISC. Keep in mind that dysfunction may be a reflection on the leader as well. Make sure that the direction is clearly communicated, team members are unblocked and supported to deliver, and they understand what their personal objectives are and how they interact with other team members.

Six-Word Lessons to Create Stellar Teams

Keeping Teams Informed Through Team Meetings

Set clear agendas for effective meetings.

Always take a few moments before a meeting to create an agenda. During a team meeting, begin by stating the agenda and what will be discussed in the meeting. The agenda can be information, update, solicitation of problem-solving ideas, etc. Managers should adhere to the agenda to ensure the efficient use of time. Discussions that don't fall under the agreed agenda should be assigned to another time.

Be on time, stay on time.

Meeting leads must have a sense of time. This means starting and adjourning the meeting on time. As convener and facilitator, the lead must ensure that discussions do not veer away from the agenda. When the team starts to digress, the person in charge must step in and redirect the discussion.

Remember that time spent on meetings should be limited; time is better spent on implementing projects.

Practice the art of note-taking.

A common mistake committed during meetings is that no one takes note of the discussions and agreements. When this happens, no one remembers what he or she is supposed to do and nothing is accomplished. A manager must assign someone from the team to take minutes of the meeting and these should be sent to all members to remind them of their tasks and responsibilities.

Listen and participate in equal amounts.

During a meeting, it's time to hear the thoughts and insights of the team members. Managers should never hog the limelight with a monologue. To have effective meetings, managers should encourage their team members to share their thoughts. Participate, acknowledge and encourage good ideas.

Recap action items and due dates.

Before closing the meeting, the lead should recap action items and assign them to team members. Every member must have a clear understanding of what he or she must do and when. It is a good idea to follow up the meeting with a recap of the action items and a schedule of activities if the tasks are numerous, interdependent and require longer term tracking.

Regularly solicit feedback about team meetings.

Feedback is important in any team and managers must regularly get feedback not only regarding the status of the projects, but also on meeting effectiveness. Besides getting ideas for meeting improvements, asking for feedback will achieve two additional objectives: it will involve and motivate the team members, and help the team lead stay on track and in sync with team thoughts.

How often should the team meet?

Team meetings are critical during the planning and implementation of projects. Proper use of time, effective facilitation, and a clear vision will guarantee that information is absorbed, and that the project implementation is successful. Managers should not organize team meetings solely to get updates from their team. Instead of meeting, the leader can "managing by walking around" and talk with team members, learning and sharing information in real time.

Contact Thomas

My goal is to remove ambiguity surrounding team dynamics. Feel free to ask questions regarding this book, or for speaking opportunities, please email me at **Thomas@T2team.com**.

Let's connect on Facebook at **facebook.com/T2TeamLLC** or visit my website at **T2Team.com**.

Thank you and best of luck with your team!

About the *Six-Word Lessons Series*

Legend has it that Ernest Hemingway was challenged to write a story using only six words. He responded with the story, "For sale: baby shoes, never worn." The story tickles the imagination. Why were the shoes never worn? The answers are left up to the reader's imagination.

This style of writing has a number of aliases: postcard fiction, flash fiction, and micro fiction. Lonnie Pacelli was introduced to this concept in 2009 by a friend, and started thinking about how this extreme brevity could apply to today's communication culture of text messages, tweets and Facebook posts. He wrote the first book, *Six-Word Lessons for Project Managers*, then started helping other authors write and publish their own books in the series.

The books all have six-word chapters with six-word lesson titles, each followed by a one-page description. They can be written by entrepreneurs who want to promote their businesses, or anyone with a message to share.

See the entire *Six-Word Lessons Series* at 6wordlessons.com

www.ingramcontent.com/pod-product-compliance
Lightning Source LLC
Chambersburg PA
CBHW070643050426
42451CB00008B/282